Realm of my life

Anupama Amudini Suresh Babu

India | USA | UK

Presentation by *BookLeaf Publishing*

Web: www.bookleafpub.com

E-mail: info@bookleafpub.com

ISBN: 9789358319491

First edition 2024

Waves and Breeze

Upon the shores of Cornwall's coast,
Where golden sands and waves make boast,
 I find myself in tranquil play,
As gentle breezes lead the way.

The salty air, a delightful kiss,
Caresses my face in sweet bliss,
With each inhale, my worries fade,
In this scenic beauty, worries are forbade.

The azure sky, a vivid hue,
Is dotted with clouds of cottony hue,
Seagulls soar on the ocean's breeze,
Their calls merging with the rustling trees.

The rhythmic crashing of the waves,
Creates a symphony nature saves,
 For those who seek its peaceful calm,
 To find serenity like a healing balm.

As I stroll along the sandy dunes,

My worries become gentle tunes,
The beach's harmony soothes my soul,
And makes me feel forever whole.

I bask in the warm embrace of the sun,
As the day slowly comes undone,
With every step, I feel at ease,
Amidst Cornwall's scenic beauty, I am pleased.

So let the breeze carry my joyous delight,
As I immerse myself in this wonderful sight,
 In Cornwall's beach, my heart does reside,
In the beauty of the scenery, I confide

"From India to UK: A Tale of Resilience and Growth

In the land of castles and ancient lore,
I ventured forth to a distant shore,
From India's embrace to UK's cold,
A tale of resilience I will unfold.

A journey embarked to a foreign land,
Where winter's grip holds with icy hand,
Amidst the snowflakes dancing in the air,
I longed for warmth and sun's golden glare.

The chill pierced through my very soul,
Adapting to the cold became my goal,
Layers upon layers, I bundled up tight,
Yet, memories of warmth brought tears to my sight.

In this new world, English became a test,
Words tangled in my tongue, unrest,
But with time and practice, I found my way,
Language no longer held me at bay.

A job, a new beginning, filled with stress,
Days full of trials, I had to confess,
As I navigated the unfamiliar terrain,

Success emerged amidst the strain.

Yet, amidst the hustle, I yearned for home,
For familiar faces, I felt so alone,
Wistful whispers echoed in my mind,
Missing loved ones I had left behind.

And oh, the taste of my favourite fare,
The spices, the flavours beyond compare,
Longing for the aromas of my mother's kitchen,
Missing the warmth of love's sweet rendition.

But in the midst of challenges and despair,
I found strength within, a flame to bear,
For I am a wanderer, resilient and bold,
A story of triumph in a foreign threshold.

With time, the cold became a companion,
The language a tool for connection,
The job a stepping stone to something more,
And memories of home, forever to adore.

So, I embrace this new country, the UK,
For it has taught me lessons along the way,
A tale of struggle, resilience, and growth,
A journey of the heart, forever I will loathe

"Solitude's Symphony: Finding Unity in Loneliness"

In a crowd, yet feeling alone,
A silent ache, my heart does bemoan.
Surrounded by faces, voices, and cheer,
But a sense of disconnect, the feeling sears.

Amidst the laughter and joyful cries,
I search for solace within their eyes.
Yet my soul finds no kinship there,
Loneliness grips me, a burden to bear.

In conversations that ebb and flow,
I yearn for a connection that I'll never know.
For buried deep, this longing resides,
To be seen and understood, a beacon outshines.

But in this sea of bustling existence,
I become an island, in isolation's distance.
Lost in a crowd, feeling adrift,
A silent plea echoes, a heartfelt rift.

Yet underneath this shroud of despair,
A whisper I hear, a gentle solace shared.
For in this moment of solitude's sting,
I realize I'm not the only one feeling.

There are others, yearning souls just like me,
Seeking solace, longing to break free.
Unified by this gnawing ache,
We meet in empathy, our loneliness awakes.

And so, dear friend, if you too feel alone,
Know there are others who may have known.
Though the crowd overwhelms, stand tall and
true,
For in the midst of everyone, I'll be there for
you.

Pause

In the flurry of life's incessant race,
A moment beckons to find a tranquil space.
Where chaos subsides and worries wane,
A pause, a respite, from the world's refrain.

Take a breath, let time slow its pace,
Embrace the stillness, find your inner grace.
For in this pause, there's solace profound,
A chance to pause, to reflect, to rebound.

No need to rush, to chase the fleeting tide,
In stillness, new perspectives reside.
Reconnect with nature, let its beauty unfold,
As worries dissolve, and peace takes hold.

In this interlude, discover wisdom's voice,
A moment's reflection, a conscious choice.
Realign your heart, let passions ignite,
In the stillness, find your truest light.

So, dear traveler, embrace this pause,
Unburden your shoulders, release life's claws.
For in the quiet, our souls come alive,
And true self-discovery begins to thrive

Resilience Unleashed

In the shadows of my teenage years,
Lies a tale of pain and shedded tears.
A journey through hardship and endless strife,
Where struggle became the rhythm of my life.

In the darkest nights, I wandered alone,
Haunted by demons I couldn't disown.
Doubt and confusion clouded my mind,
Leaving scars on my soul, difficult to find.

The weight of expectations, a burden so deep,
Crushing my spirit, numbing my sleep.
Insecurities echoed in every step,
Leaving me feeling lost, like I had nothing kept.

But amidst the chaos, a spark ignited,
A flame within me, unwilling to be slighted.
With every fall, I learned to rise,
To brave the pain and reach for the skies.

Each struggle endured, a lesson was learned,
Building resilience, inner strength earned.
Through the trials and tribulations I faced,
My spirit grew, leaving no trace of waste.

So, here I stand, scars and all,
A testament to the battles that made me stand
tall.
Teenage pain has shaped who I am,
A warrior, a survivor, strong as a ram.

No longer defined by the struggles I've known,
But empowered by the strength I've honed.
For the pain I endured, I am grateful, you see,
For it taught me resilience and set my spirit free

Against All Odds, I Rise

In a world where odds seem stacked,
Against my dreams, against the fact,
That lack of money and support may be,
Barriers standing tall in front of me.

With empty pockets and a longing heart,
I face the challenges, ready to chart,
A path of resilience, against the tide,
Where perseverance becomes my guide.

Lack of money, a weight that pulls,
But determination fuels my soul with goals.
I'll scrape and save, work day and night,
To pursue my dreams, to reach new heights.

Without a home or a familiar place,
I find solace in the strength I embrace.
For family may not be defined by blood,
But by those who uplift and understand.

Their support may be absent, yet I persist,
With unwavering hope, love in my fist.
For in the face of adversity's cruel test,
I'll fight and strive, I won't settle for less.

Against all odds, I stand tall and strong,
Defying the naysayers, proving them wrong.
For dreams don't discriminate, they're for all,
No matter how circumstances may befall.

I'll build my own foundation, brick by brick,
With determination and a purpose that sticks.
For in the struggle, resilience is born,
A spirit unyielding, weathered but not torn.

With every step forward, obstacles in my way,
I'll gather strength, shedding doubt like decay.
For it's in the darkness, the challenges we face,
That we find our true selves, our destined place.

So, I embrace the odds, I'll fight with might,
With passion as my armor, I'll shine a light.
For in the face of adversity's fierce storm,
I'll rise above, resilient and transformed

Unbreakable Bonds: A Love Beyond Blood

In a world where bonds are formed,
By love and not just blood,
There lie two precious souls,
Who call me "Aunty" with affection and trust.

Though not related by birth,
Our connection runs deep,
For they are not just nieces to me,
But treasured friends I keep.

Their laughter, like sweet melodies,
Bringing joy to everyday,
Their smiles, like beams of sunshine,
Illuminate my life in every way.

We share secrets and stories,
Build castles in the air,
With them, I feel complete,
Knowing they will always be there.

Love knows no boundaries,
And family extends beyond blood,
For in these two precious souls,
I found a love that's pure and good.

So, to my nieces who are not related by blood,
Yet hold a special place in my heart,
Know that I am forever grateful,
For the love and friendship we impart

Fleeting Shadows: Emotions Between Worlds

The streets alive with vibrant sounds, a
symphony of the unknown,
Each corner holds a secret, waiting to be shown.
The taste of exotic flavors, a feast upon the
tongue,
But still, a hunger for familiarity, a yearning left
unsung.

The beauty of the foreign land, in every sight
and sound,
Leaves me both enchanted and adrift, in feelings
so profound.
The thrill of exploration, the thrill of the
unknown,
But a longing for the comfort of the place I've
always known.

The language dances on my ears, a melody so
new,
But echoes of my mother tongue, remind me of
what's true.
The customs and traditions, intriguing and
unknown,

Yet a longing for the rituals, the familiar that I've
grown.

The bonds forged with new-found friends, like
branches reaching wide,
Bring warmth and joy in foreign lands, where
hearts begin to glide.
But a tugging at my heartstrings, a void I can't
ignore,
As thoughts of loved ones left behind, occupy
my core.

In foreign lands, a dichotomy, where mixed
emotions play,
As I navigate the uncharted path, each and every
day.
Embracing the adventure, while missing what
I've known,
A bittersweet reminder that my heart is never
fully grown.

So I carry with me fragments, of both worlds
intertwined,
The joys and longings coexisting, in a tapestry
undefined.
For in this mixture of emotions, I find growth
and empathy,
As I learn to bridge the distance between what
was and what will be.

Whispers of the Compassionate: A Social Worker's Journey

In a world of compassion, where hearts are weighed,
A social worker's path is carefully laid.
To bring hope and solace, to ease every strife,
But within this noble role, exists a work-life.

Under the weight of responsibilities and care,
A social worker faces burdens hard to bear.
The pressure is a constant, the demands are high,
Balancing it all, they often wonder why.

With empathy as their guiding light,
They lend a helping hand in the darkest night.
But their own strength falters, as exhaustion
looms,
In the face of struggle, they carry heavy gloom.

The stories they hear like a heavy flood,
Leaving a lasting mark, like a crimson blood.
Each talk, each tear, takes a piece of their soul,
Yet they press on, for their purpose is their goal.

In the face of adversity, they find their might,
To create change, to bring about the light.
They advocate fiercely for those who can't,
Amidst the challenges, they simply can't relent.

But oh, the battles that wage within,
The emotional toll as they witness sin.
The weight of the world rests upon their
shoulder,
As they fight for justice, they only grow bolder.

Yet, in the midst of this relentless grind,
A social worker's heart will always find,
That the impact they make, the lives they touch,
Makes it all worthwhile, it means so much.

So let us honor the social worker's plight,
For they endure the pressures with all their
might.
May we support them and lend a helping hand,
For they work tirelessly to make this world
grand

Beneath the Veil of Darkness

In the shadows of a weary soul,
Depression takes its heavy toll.
A weight that anchors deep within,
A battle where darkness always seems to win.

Invisible chains, they grip so tight,
Draining both day and sleepless night.
A cloud of despair, that lingers near,
Distorting thoughts, igniting fear.

The sun's warm embrace feels far away,
As heaviness lingers, day after day.
A constant struggle, like a turbulent sea,
Fighting against a current that won't set free.

Simple tasks turn into mountains to climb,
And laughter becomes a distant chime.
A loss of joy, once so brightly felt,
Replaced by emptiness, a heart that dwells.

But in this fight, remember you're strong,
Though it may seem the battle is lifelong.
Reach out for help, let your voice be heard,
For together we can surmount this difficult
word.

With open hearts, we'll stand by your side,
Offering love, support, and a place to confide.
In the depths of despair, there is still hope,
A glimmer of light, a way to cope.

Seek the hand of therapy, the guiding light,
To illuminate a path through darkest night.
Medicine and self-care, tools to fight,
To reclaim your strength, to shine so bright.

Remember, dear soul, you are not alone,
In this journey, compassion is shown.
Your struggle is real, your pain is true,
But healing is possible, and it waits for you.

So, as you navigate the depths of this sea,
Let resilience and hope be your decree.
You are worthy of love, of joy, and peace,
And with time and support, the storm will cease

Soul's Symphony: Unveiling the Journey

In the realm of my existence, a unique story
unfolds,
A vibrant soul with tales yet to be told.
With each passing moment and every step I take,
The essence of who I am, begins to awake.

Within my heart, a universe resides,
A myriad of dreams and passions that guides.
My journey, a tapestry woven with grace,
Filled with experiences that time can't erase.

I've faced challenges with unwavering might,
Overcoming obstacles that blocked my sight.
In times of weakness, I've found inner strength,
Drawing courage from within, at any length.

My resilience, a beacon in the darkest hour,
A testament to my unwavering power.
Through joy and sorrow, laughter and tears,
I've crafted a symphony that echoes through the
years.

In the depths of my being, wisdom takes root,
A wellspring of knowledge, a resolute pursuit.

With an open mind, I seek to understand,
The mysteries of life, the wonders at hand.

My dreams unfold like petals in bloom,
Embracing passions that bring my spirit to
zoom.
Whether in pursuit of knowledge or creative
pursuits,
My endeavors shine, creating beautiful fruits.

In the tapestry of human existence, I play a part,
A unique thread weaving its way into the art.
So, I embrace the story I weave,
For within me lies the power to achieve.

I embrace my quirks, my flaws, my hopes,
For it is through my journey, beauty elopes.
I am a shining light, a constellation in the sky,
A masterpiece in progress, with endless potential
nigh.

Mind Held Strong: Defying the Chaos

In the depths of the chaotic storm,
Where thoughts collide and emotions swarm,
I feel the weight upon my chest,
The fear that I may lose my best.

A torrent of doubts engulfs my soul,
Threatening to consume me, to take control,
But deep within, a flicker remains,
A steadfast spirit that refuses to wane.

I hold onto the fragments of my sanity,
Clutching tightly, never losing grip, you see,
For in this battle, I'll stand tall and brave,
Even when it feels like I'm on the edge of a
grave.

Though the darkness whispers in my ear,
I'll shield my mind, refusing to give in to fear,
With each passing moment, I'll endure,
For my strength lies in my will to be sure.

When the world around me seems askew,
I'll hold fast to the thoughts that are true,
For in this journey, I shall find,

That I possess the power to heal my mind.

So, I rise above the doubts that entwine,
Knowing that my spirit will always shine,
In the face of uncertainty, I remain strong,
Holding onto my mind, where I belong.

And though the tempest may try to sway,
I'll stay grounded, come what may,
For in this battle, my faith will abide,
Holding on to my mind, deep inside.

Eternal Nomad: Love and Passion of a World Traveler

Oh, the wanderlust that stirs within my soul,
A burning passion that yearns to be whole.
For the world is vast, a treasure unexplored,
And I, a traveler, forever eager and adored.

With every step, a new horizon unfurls,
A tapestry woven with wonders and pearls.
From ancient ruins to vibrant cultures alive,
Traveling the world, my heart will survive.

I chase the sunsets, with golden hues ablaze,
Embracing unknown lands, in awe and amaze.
Through bustling streets and tranquil shores,
I find beauty in every place my feet explore.

The taste of local flavors upon my lips,
The melody of languages, like sweet whispered
tricks.
The touch of history, in ancient walls and stones,
I'm bound to this longing, wherever it roams.

In each encounter, connections are found,
Sharing stories and laughter, profound.
For as I journey, my heart opens wide,

Embracing humanity on this global ride.

The world is my canvas, an artist's dream,
With every destination, a new masterpiece
gleams.
For in the depths of wanderlust's embrace,
I find solace, joy, and a sense of grace.

So, I set forth, with adventurous delight,
To explore the world, both day and night.
For the love and passion I hold so dear,
Traveling the world, forever brings me near.

Whispers of Love

In the depths of my heart, a silent ache resides,
A love so profound, but concealed it hides.
Words gather on my tongue, yet fail to escape,
Like timid butterflies, afraid to take shape.

In the canvas of my mind, emotions painted
bold,
But their colors fade, their stories remain untold.
For fear grips my courage, denying me the
chance,
To express the affection in a loving dance.

Through stolen glances and subtle gestures,
I long to reach out, to reveal what my heart
whispers.
But a prison of uncertainty holds me captive,
Leaving my soul stranded in a loveless narrative.

The stars above witness my inner plight,
As I yearn to bask in your radiant light.
Yet, silence wraps around me like a shroud,
As my unspoken love remains buried in a cloud.

Oh, if only words could bridge this divide,
And unlock the affection I desperately hide.

But alas, my love, you may never know,
The depths of my emotions I dare not show.

And so, with a heavy heart, I silently endure,
The agony of a love that may never mature.
But know, dear one, though these words may not
be spoken,
In my heart forever, your love will be unbroken

Unleashed: From Darkness to Empowerment

Through trials faced, a difficult trail,
A past of shadows, where strength did prevail.
In the depths of struggle, I found my might,
Empowered to rise, to embrace the light.

Each step, a lesson, etched deep within,
A journey of growth, where strength would begin.
From shattered pieces, I built anew,
A foundation sturdy, resilient and true.

The wounds that once bled, now scars of grace,
Reminders of battles fought in this sacred space.
The storms that raged, the challenges faced,
Forged a spirit, unyielding and unchased.

In the face of doubt, I found my voice,
Unleashing the power, my truest choice.
I stood tall, with courage in my core,
Embracing my worth, forevermore.

No longer defined by mistakes or strife,
I walk this path, freer in this life.
For every obstacle, a chance to grow,

To bloom from darkness, where strength would
flow.

From the ashes, a phoenix will rise,
A testament to the soul's endless skies.
I paint my own canvas, colors so bold,
Empowered, awakened, the story unfolds.

With each scar and wound, I have overcome,
I reclaim my power, where strength cannot be
undone.
The path that I've traveled, paved with
resilience,
A testament to the spirit's brilliance.

So let the past be a stepping stone,
A source of wisdom, to call my own.
I embrace the journey, the highs and lows,
Empowered, transformed, my true self shows.

The Radiant Flatmate: Dreams, Shopping, and Flavors"

In our cozy flat, where life intertwines,
Resides a flatmate, with passions that shine.
From sleepy slumbers to shopping sprees,
A life full of flavor and vibrant dreams.

With each day's end, they seek their retreat,
To cozy pillows and soft sheets they fleet.
In dreamland's embrace, they find their bliss,
Wrapped in tranquility, a sweet abyss.

But as the sun rises, a new day begins,
Adventures await, an eager spirit within.
They love to shop, exploring every store,
Finding treasures aplenty, they always want
more.

From fashionable clothes to stylish shoes,
Their wardrobe sparkles, vibrant hues.
In love with orange, a color so bright,
It ignites their passion, a pure delight.

And when it comes to scrumptious cuisine,

Their taste buds twinkle, a gastronomic scene.
They savor each bite, flavors rich and pure,
In food's embrace, their happiness sure.

From chocolaty desserts to spicy delights,
They indulge with pleasure, day and night.
Exploring flavors, the culinary unknown,
Their love for good food brightly shown.

In our shared space, their presence blooms,
An energy vibrant, filling every room.
With their warm smile and zest for life,
They inspire us all, banishing strife.

Oh, dear flatmate, with joys untold,
Your passions ignite, your spirit bold.
May sleep bring you dreams of wonder and
peace,
While shopping and food nourish your lease.

And as we gather beneath our cozy roof,
Our bonds grow stronger, each day a proof.
For you, dear flatmate, bring joy and zest,
A vibrant presence, simply the best.

Solitude's Song: Longing for Companionship

In solitude, I find my peace, a respite for my soul,
Yet in the depths of silence, there lingers a longing, a whispering call.
The desire to wander, free and unattached, holds me in its sway,
But even in my solitude, I yearn for someone to be by my side, someday.

To walk amidst the whispering trees, in nature's tranquil grace,
To revel in the solitude, with a companion, face to face.
In solitude, I find solace, a chance to reflect and mend,
But still, my heart grows restless, longing for a companion, a friend.

The stars above, they twinkle bright, a blanket in the sky,
Their distant glow, a gentle reminder, of a love I hope to find.
To share the quiet moments, the stolen glances and warm embrace,

In solitude I'll find my strength, but together
we'll find a different space.

To cherish each other's thoughts, in the peaceful
seclusion we'll reside,
The comfort of a hand to hold, as we journey
side by side.
In solitude, I'll find my calm, but in your
presence, a new song,
For togetherness and solitude can harmonize and
both belong.

So while I seek solace in my moments of
serenity and grace,
I hold onto the hope that one day, you'll find
your way to this place.
To be alone, yet not lonely, with a heart that's
full and wide,
In solitude, I'll find my solace, but alongside
you, I'll find my stride.

"Blooming Excitement: A New Niece or Nephew Awaits

In anticipation's tender grasp, I wait with bated breath,
For the arrival of a little one, a new life to be blessed.
My brother's child soon to be born, a niece or nephew dear,
The joy that swells within my heart, undying and sincere.

With every passing day and night, excitement fills the air,
Imagining their tiny face, their presence everywhere.
The dreams and hopes, the endless possibilities they'll hold,
A precious gift from heaven's grace, a miracle to behold.

I envision playful laughter, shared moments full of glee,
Adventures and traditions, woven through our family tree.

As I await their precious arrival, my heart grows
bigger still,
For the love I have yet to give, and the joy they
will instill.

I'll be the guide, the confidant, a pillar they can
lean on,
Supporting dreams and aspirations, until they've
fully grown.
In their eyes, I'll see a reflection of our shared
bloodline,
A bond that's forged forever, a love that's so
divine.

So as I eagerly anticipate, each passing day that
goes,
I'll cherish this sweet waiting time, as love
within me grows.
For soon a new chapter will begin, for brother,
child, and me,
To welcome this precious little one, a bundle of
joy, to be

Mystic Highlands: A Journey Through Scotland's Beauty

In the land of tartans and ancient lore,
Where misty mountains and rugged shores,
Scotland's beauty unfolds, like a painter's dream,
A land so enchanting, it makes the heart gleam.

Stretched across majestic highlands and glens,
A wilderness unfolds, untouched and untamed,
Heather-clad hills, a tapestry of purple and
green,
A breathtaking vista, like none ever seen.

Lochs sparkling like gemstones, crystal clear,
Reflecting the sky, so serene and near,
From Loch Lomond to Ness, their waters
embrace,
Mysteries unravel, with every ripple's trace.

Castles stand proud, steeped in history's
embrace,
Guardians of tales, of battles fought with grace,
Edinburgh Castle atop its volcanic throne,
A sentinel watching, where legends were sown.

The Isle of Skye, with its fairy tale charm,

Where rugged cliffs and waterfalls disarm,
Quiraing and Old Man of Storr, mystical heights,
With each breathtaking view, the soul takes flight.

From Glen Coe's haunting valley, steeped in pain,
To the Isle of Arran, where tranquility reigns,
Scotland's landscapes evoke emotions untold,
A testament to nature's beauty untrolled.

And in its people, warm hearts beat strong,
Kindness and hospitality, a Scottish song,
Poets and musicians, expressing the soul,
Their words and melodies, a beauty uncontrolled.

Oh, Scotland, your beauty is a sight to behold,
From highland glens to tales of old,
A land of castles, mountains, and lore,
Forever capturing hearts, forever wanting more

Solitude Amidst the Crowd

In the bustling crowd I stand alone,
Surrounded by faces, yet feeling unknown.
Amidst the laughter and lively chatter,
I can't shake this feeling, it doesn't matter.

The pain of distance weighs heavy on my heart,
From my homeland, I'm thousands of miles
apart.
Memories of familiar sights and sounds,
Now distant echoes that no longer resound.

Lost in the sea of unfamiliar faces,
Longing for the warmth of familiar places.
I yearn for the solace of my home,
Where my roots are deep, where I belong.

Though surrounded by people, I feel detached,
An invisible wall around me, unmatched.
Bleak loneliness engulfs me like a shroud,
Leaving me longing for a familiar cloud.

But in this moment of desolate despair,
I find solace in knowing that others also share,
The pain of being adrift in a foreign land,
Seeking connection, a comforting hand.

For in this vast world, we're not alone,
Others carry homesickness, this I've known.
And together we unite, finding strength in our
plight,
To bring light to the darkness, and make all
things right.

So let us embrace one another in our pain,
Shield each other from the loneliness, like
pouring rain.
And though far from home, we'll find our way,
In the midst of many, we will find solace and
stay

Enchanted Christmas: Nights, Lights, and Markets in the UK

Beneath a velvet winter sky, the Christmas nights a stage,
The UK dressed in festive lights, heritage and age.
In hallowed squares and cobbled streets the yuletide markets bloom,
With holly wreaths and sprigs of fir, interlaced with pine perfume.

The carolers in cozy wraps sing notes that rise and fall,
Enchantment hangs upon the air; it beckons one and all.
The Christmas lights, like faerie dust, cascade on every face,
A milky way on earthly ground, a celestial embrace.

Each market stall's a treasure trove, with baubles glinting bright,
Hand-crafted gifts and gingerbread, candles casting light.

Mulled cider warms the winter chill, steam rises
in the cold,
While children laugh and couples stroll, new
memories unfold.

The ferris wheels and merry-go's, add to the
festive cheer,
Their silhouettes against night skies, music to
the ear.
The echoes of "Auld Lang Syne" are softly in
the breeze,
So join the dance and sing along, with boundless
festive ease.

The lights reflect in children's eyes, filled with
wonder, gleam,
As pudding, mince pies, and treats galore, are
part of Christmas dream.
The Big Ben chimes its timeless song, a
reminder of the past,
Where every moment here tonight, in memories
will last.

In Gloucester, Bristol, or London's heart,
wherever you may roam,
Each Christmas market under lights will make
you feel at home.
From North to South, in winter's grip, the
kingdom wears its crown,

Of Christmas nights and market lights, in every town it's known

42